Deer

by Derek Zobel

BELLWETHER MEDIA • MINNEAPOLIS, MN

Note to Librarians, Teachers, and Parents:

Blastoff! Readers are carefully developed by literacy experts and combine standards-based content with developmentally appropriate text.

Level 1 provides the most support through repetition of high-frequency words, light text, predictable sentence patterns, and strong visual support.

Level 2 offers early readers a bit more challenge through varied simple sentences, increased text load, and less repetition of high-frequency words.

Level 3 advances early-fluent readers toward fluency through increased text and concept load, less reliance on visuals, longer sentences, and more literary language.

Level 4 builds reading stamina by providing more text per page, increased use of punctuation, greater variation in sentence patterns, and increasingly challenging vocabulary.

Level 5 encourages children to move from "learning to read" to "reading to learn" by providing even more text, varied writing styles, and less familiar topics.

Whichever book is right for your reader, Blastoff! Readers are the perfect books to build confidence and encourage a love of reading that will last a lifetime!

This edition first published in 2011 by Bellwether Media, Inc.

No part of this publication may be reproduced in whole or in part without written permission of the publisher. For information regarding permission, write to Bellwether Media, Inc., Attention: Permissions Department, 5357 Penn Avenue South, Minneapolis, MN 55419.

Library of Congress Cataloging-in-Publication Data
Zobel, Derek, 1983–
  Deer / by Derek Zobel.
    p. cm. – (Blastoff! readers. Backyard wildlife)
  Includes bibliographical references and index.
  Summary: "Developed by literacy experts for students in kindergarten through grade three, this book introduces deer to young readers through leveled text and related photos"–Provided by publisher.
  ISBN 978-1-60014-440-0 (hardcover : alk. paper)
  1. Deer–Juvenile literature. I. Title.
QL737.U55Z63 2010
599.65–dc22   2010010682

Text copyright © 2011 by Bellwether Media, Inc. BLASTOFF! READERS and associated logos are trademarks and/or registered trademarks of Bellwether Media, Inc.

Printed in the United States of America, North Mankato, MN.

080110   1162

Contents

Deer are animals
with skinny legs
and big bodies.
They live in forests
and grasslands.

Deer run very quickly.
They are also good
swimmers and jumpers.

Deer have a **hoof** on each foot. Each hoof has four toes.

hoof

Deer scrape the
ground with
their hooves.
They leave a
scent behind
that keeps
other deer away.

Deer have big eyes. They see at night as well as they do during the day.

Deer eat grass,
fruits, and nuts
in the summer.
They eat bark and
twigs in the winter.

Male deer are called **bucks**. Female deer are called **does**.

buck

doe

17

Bucks grow **antlers** every year. They rub their antlers against trees.

Bucks use their antlers to fight for land. They also fight for does. Watch out!

Glossary

antlers—bones that come out of the head of a buck

bucks—male deer

does—female deer

hoof—a hard covering that a deer has on each foot

scent—the smell of an animal

To Learn More

AT THE LIBRARY

Evert, Laura. *Whitetail Deer*. Minnetonka, Minn.: NorthWord Press, 2000.

Sams, Carl R., and Jean Stoick. *Lost in the Woods: A Photographic Fantasy*. Milford, Mich.: C.R. Sams II Photography, 2004.

Wilder, Laura Ingalls. *The Deer in the Wood*. New York, N.Y.: HarperCollins, 1995.

ON THE WEB

Learning more about deer is as easy as 1, 2, 3.

1. Go to www.factsurfer.com.

2. Enter "deer" into the search box.

3. Click the "Surf" button and you will see a list of related Web sites.

With factsurfer.com, finding more information is just a click away.

Index